Published by
Peppermint Toast Publishing
New Westminster, British Columbia
www.peppermintoast.com

Editing by Grayson Smith
Design by Kristin Church

Printed by Hemlock Printers,
British Columbia, Canada

FSC
www.fsc.org

MIX
Paper from
responsible sources
FSC® C014956

I was born
Precious
and **Sacred**

ACKNOWLEDGEMENTS

The Victoria Native Friendship Centre wishes to acknowledge the Traditional Territory of the Lekwammen People, known today as the Songhees Nation and Esquimalt Nation. We humbly offer our sincere gratitude to the Elders, Chiefs, and People of these territories for their gracious hospitality and for allowing us to live, work and play on their beautiful land.

The Victoria Native Friendship Centre offers our deepest gratitude to the Elders, children, youth, parents, VNFC staff and all of the Community who contributed so generously in the creation of our book, including the following:

- Francis Dick of the Kwakwaka'wakw Nation for the original "I Was Born Precious and Sacred" art work.

- SAGAcom for photography.

- The Ministry of Children and Family Development for the generous financial contribution which supported the publication of this book.

Jenna Rae Photography, Regina, SK

This book is dedicated to my Precious brother Dwight,
and his Sacred grand baby Eli.

I was born **Precious** and **Sacred**...

...and this **I need to know.**

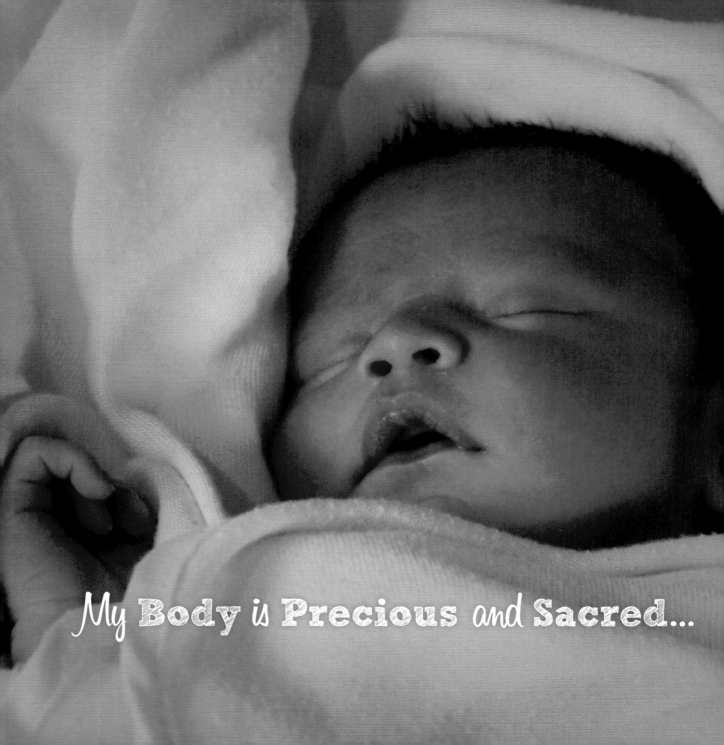

My Body is Precious and Sacred...

...and this I need to know.

My Heart is Precious and Sacred...

...and this I need to know.

My Spirit is Precious and Sacred...

...and this I need to know.

My Mind is Precious and Sacred...

...and this I need to know.

All of Me is Precious and Sacred...

...and this I need to know.

...and this I need to know.

People who love me in safe
and healthy ways
know that I am Precious and Sacred...

...and this I need to know.

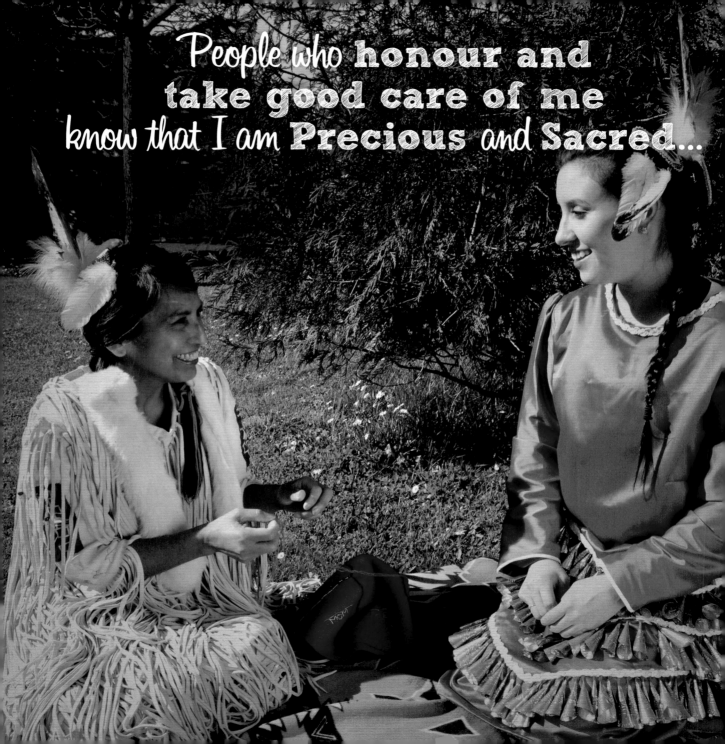

People who honour and take good care of me know that I am **Precious** and **Sacred...**

...and this I need to know.

People who understand that
I am a gift in this world
know that I am Precious and Sacred...

...and this I need to know.

I was born Precious and Sacred...

I am Precious and Sacred...

...and this I now know.